Lives Upside Down

Surviving Divorce

UNDERSTANDING THE EFFECTS OF DIVORCE
ON ADULTS AND CHILDREN

by James V. Flosi

ACTA Publications
Chicago, Illinois

LIVES UPSIDE DOWN
SURVIVING DIVORCE
by James V. Flosi, D.Min.

Edited by
Gregory F. Augustine Pierce

Typography by
Garrison Publications

Cover Design by
Monaco/Viola Incorporated

Copyright © 1993: ACTA Publications
                   4848 N. Clark Street
                   Chicago, Illinois 60640
                   (312) 271-1030

Library of Congress Catalog Number: 93-070521

ISBN: 0-87946-083-0

Printed in the United States of America

CONTENTS

Bob's Story   I

Part I: The Effects of Divorce on the Couple Themselves

Introduction   9

Chapter I: The Questioning Stage   II

Do I Really Want to Continue This
Relationship?
   • Sylvia's Story
   • Reflection

Chapter 2: The Escape Stage   19

How Do I Say It's Over?
   • Martha's Story
   • Reflection

Chapter 3: The Transition Stage   27

Why Are the Walls Closing in on Me?
   • David's Story
   • Reflection

Chapter 4: The Rediscovery Stage   41

I Feel, for the First Time, That I Am
Living My Own Life.
   • Ann's Story
   • Reflection

Part II: The Effects of Divorce on the Couple's Children

Introduction   51

Chapter 5: The Child's Questioning Stage 55

Why Are Things Beginning to Change
in Our Family?
- Mark's Story
- Reflection

Chapter 6: The Child's Anti-Escape Stage 61

How Do I Get Mom and Dad to Talk to One
Another Again?
- Renee's Story
- Reflection

Chapter 7: The Child's Transition Stage   67

No Voice, No Choice.
- Tom's Story
- Reflection

Chapter 8: The Child's Rediscovery Stage 83

Will My Parents' History Repeat Itself?
- Patricia's Story
- Reflection

Dedication

To John and Ann, my parents,
who lived the ups and downs
of marriage and survived with
forgiveness and constant love.

Thank You

Faith Kofink, Nan Gold, O.S.B., and
Eunice Dohra, who made this book
possible with their talents, advice,
and refinements.

To the thousands of people who
have taught me how to express
their divorcing stories with
understanding and compassion.

And finally to three very supportive
journeymates, my sister, Olivia
Stukel, Antoinette Perrone and Bob
Viola, for their love and support.

BOB'S STORY

Like many other late spring days, this one smelled of early summer heat and dying lilacs. It was a day that seemed ordinary, but it became one I will never forget. It was a day that changed my life.

It's funny the way bad things affect us. They seem to be all we can remember at the worst of times. They eat away at us if we let them. But bad things can bring good, too, if we let them.

I was revisiting my old neighborhood—the one I had lived in all of my young life—on that day in early June of 1957. I was only 11, but on that day I grew up forever.

The old neighborhood always looked the same to me when I returned to visit (which was as often as I could), but that day it took on a special excitement. I was getting together with some friends to play ball, and I had been anticipating the game for a long time. School was out, and I was finally relieved from the stress and confusion caused by having changed schools in mid-year. I was excited and free and longed to be with friends on familiar ground.

My first stop was to meet my best friend, Bob Johnson. I remember going to his apartment building and walking up the dark, narrow stairwell to the third-floor landing, lit by a solitary, naked light bulb. It might have looked eerie and spooky to me, except for the fact that I had been there a million times before. As always, the wooden door was painted dark brown "so as not to show the dirt" as Bob's mom always explained.

Above the door was a glass transom that had come in handy many times over the past couple of years. You see, Bob's folks had divorced two years before, and he had since been living with his mom and her new husband, who just didn't seem to understand Bob and, I knew, didn't like me. So the transom was a good way to sneak out—and in—when Bob was "grounded," which was often.

I knocked on the door, hoping that Bob, not one of his parents, would answer. Silence. I knocked again, but still the door stayed shut. I looked up at the transom. This, too, remained tightly closed. I remembered the times when I had brought some of my clothes for Bob in a brown paper bag. When Mrs. Johnson's new husband got angry at Bob for having done something wrong or for not having done anything at all, he would take Bob's clothes and lock them in the closet and then rig the door in some way so that he would know if it had been opened during the day. (We never did find out how he did that.) So I would knock on the brown door and Bob would open the transom, grab my bag of clothes, put them on, and crawl out of the transom.

We were always lucky enough to get back and reverse our actions just before his stepfather returned from work.

This day, however, neither door nor transom opened, so I retraced my steps back down the three flights of stairs to the sun-drenched entrance and walked outside. I sat on the curb for awhile, periodically looking up at the window of Bob's apartment, hoping he was really there and just playing a game with me. I wanted so badly to get to the park, but I didn't want to go without him. As I sat there, I recalled the many questions Bob had asked me during those past two or three years—questions about family, about feeling guilty, about hurting, and about not liking his new way of life. The continuous litany of searching questions were too deep and too complex for me to answer. Our teachers were not much help at answering them, either. You see, at that time divorce was an exception.

I finally went to the park that day by myself. It was a good day. Walking back home about five o'clock in the afternoon, sweaty and tired, all I could think of was a cold glass of Kool-Aid. As I turned the corner near my grandfather's store, I saw my father sitting by himself on the stoop, watching for me. He waited until I was close to him and quietly asked me to sit down beside him. I don't remember his first sentence, but I do recall his tear-glazed eyes and the piece of paper that he handed to me. It was a note from Bob. I didn't understand. I read the note. It said that Bob was sorry, he was not going to the park today, and that all he wanted was to be happy, and that he was sorry if I was hurt, and that he was saying good-bye. I didn't understand the note, and I must have looked fearful and confused. My father took me in his arms and told me in a whisper that Bob was found dead that day . . . that he had hanged himself. And I still didn't understand.

This story, with all its repercussions, was the reason and starting point for my involvement in the lives of countless divorced and separated people who have felt alienated and confused because of their personal situation. The lack of knowledgeable, supportive counselors to help Bob's mom and her new husband ease Bob through his difficult times and the lack of knowledgeable, supportive teachers to spot Bob's depression and identify its cause have channeled my energies as a pastoral counselor. I have tried my best to change the environment and experience of all the aching, broken, separated, and divorcing people and their children I have encountered since my friend Bob died over 35 years ago.

Bob's story has taken its place in my memory as a symbol for all the other stories I have heard. I will tell and reflect upon some of these stories in this book to help you understand that there are common threads for those experiencing divorce and separation, and for their children, no matter how diverse the circumstances might appear. Every marital breakup is different, of course, but in some ways they are all the same.

Divorce is survivable—both for the couple themselves and for their children. I hope these stories and reflections will ease some of your pain, facilitate your counseling, and even make you laugh at the crazy things you do to survive.

Part I

THE EFFECTS OF DIVORCE ON

THE COUPLE THEMSELVES

INTRODUCTION

Divorcing is a process, not just a piece of paper. Divorcing can mean years of agony and battle, or it can be a period of time in which two people dispassionately begin to reorganize their priorities and decide that their individual lives do not include each other anymore. Divorcing can be a roller coaster of ups and downs, with rushes of fear and guilt followed by moments of peace and relief. Divorcing can be hell, or it can be the beginning of a vibrant and directioned life.

How two people divorce lays the foundation and structure for their subsequently tragic or successful lives. It also can mean the difference between continuing the cycle of control and manipulation of each other or beginning the process of each person taking control of his or her own life and moving forward. How a person divorces, in some cases, can literally determine the difference between death and life.

Divorcing people often ask: "Am I ever going to get through this hell?" The answer is, of course, "It depends." For each malicious act of revenge or hate that one throws into the divorcing process, it will be that much harder to get over the divorcing. Adults who manipulate and delay the divorcing process because of their desperation and false hopes need to come, finally, to the conclusion that it is over. Until that time, the hell that is being experienced will almost certainly continue.

Adults, on the other hand, who learn at least the basic outline of the divorcing process given here, will be somewhat aware of the stumbling blocks that most people encounter. This will enable them to plan accordingly. Being aware and being able to plan may not change the process. But these two elements provide some control over the environment in which the divorcing process takes place. This might mean for some the difference between maintaining sanity and "going over the edge."

Divorce is survivable for adults. If hate and "getting even" gradually disappear from the process, forgiveness and control of one's own life start taking over. If the hurt and loss are handled right, then the two individuals will be better equipped to enter their new lives not being controlled by their former spouse or by any other outside influences.

Here, then, are stories and reflections on the four stages of divorce that I have observed over and over among divorcing couples and the effects that each phase has on the couples themselves.

CHAPTER 1

THE QUESTIONING STAGE

DO I REALLY WANT TO CONTINUE IN THIS RELATIONSHIP?

Sylvia's Story

Jack and I were married for 32 years. To most people, our marriage seemed ideal. Both of us were well-educated, successful, and possessed a keen sense of community-mindedness. Jack was a very successful lawyer, and I was a civic-minded wife and mother of two. Both of us were socially mature at the time of our wedding and continued as a mutual support for each other in many of the projects we undertook.

So it was a complete shock when one day Jack told me that he wanted a divorce. This announcement was totally unexpected and devastating. At least I thought so then. For the ten years following that marital decision I swore I never had an inkling

of what was going on in Jack's mind. It is only
recently, as I look back and am not afraid to search
out answers, that I can admit that, if I had let myself,
I'd have seen it coming all along. Jack, on the other
hand, can pick out the day when he started questioning his involvement in the marriage and his need to
"recapture lost time and lost experiences." He
remembers the first years of our marriage in which
he and I forcibly adjusted to each other—those were
the days when "working out problems" was the only
option available to people with marital difficulties—
as especially harsh. I thought we had merely the
ordinary difficulties of two independent people
getting accustomed to sharing space and privacy.
During our first year and a half, I felt we were
basically happy and concerned for each other. But,
in any case, our conscious concern for being husband and wife gave way as soon as I became preg-
nant with our first child. We were happy and
content to start a family and to give it everything we
could, and we put our marital problems on the back
burner.

This vocation of parenting intensified after our
second child. It drew us further into a way of life
that had only one set of concerns—the health,

education, and future of our children. The thing we did not realize was that we were robbing ourselves of the most important relationship we possessed— our relationship as husband and wife.

Jack started to feel something missing only after the children were grown. Our daughter had already married and our son was in the midst of planning his wedding. Jack had not really felt anything for me in a long time. The only communication that survived those years centered on children, work, and outside involvement. There were no intimacies, excitement, or direction in our new situation, which was as "parents without live-in children."

Jack had decided long ago that things just weren't right between us, but because the children were the center of his life and mine, our marriage had taken second place. He worked hard and long to make sure that the children were successfully raised before he began to reconsider our relationship, and then he started diligently working toward the ending of our marriage.

Reflection

Sensitive observers agree that divorcing is a process, not just a certificate received when litigation is completed. Divorce is a long, difficult, and often devastating human experience. When two people who have loved each other deeply for a period of time become caught up with each other's uncertainties, dissatisfactions, and continuous lack of communication, the divorcing process begins.

Sylvia's story contains just one scenario for this questioning stage. But no matter how long a couple has been married, or what the quality of their relationship has been, the divorce process starts when usually one, sometimes both, partners begin to question the very basis of their union.

The most important relationship in a family is the spousal relationship. For a couple to be husband and wife to each other is the essence of the family role model for children. Being a parent, which is also significant, should be of secondary importance. It is obvious that being a parent is time-, energy-, and interest-consuming. But so is being a spouse. A model of family is needed in which husband and wife can develop within themselves and each other a lifestyle which gives priority to their spousal relationship and, at the same time, helps to develop their children's personalities in a healthy way.

In the questioning stage of the divorcing experience, the issue is investment. In this phase, contentment—the peaceful acceptance of the status quo—turns to discontent and often the discontent leads to the inevitable question: Do I really want to continue in this relationship? Usually only one of the partners begins the deliberation of the pros and cons of the marital stalemate, trying to figure out whether it's worth continuing to invest in or not. Put in its simplest terms, the question is: Do I want to invest any more time (energy, sex, money) in something that I feel is not going anywhere? This questioning stage necessitates distance, sometimes physical as well as emotional. It is the phase when one of the two partners finds it necessary to spend time by himself or herself (or in the company of others) thinking about the marital relationship and evaluating it.

What ensues is an up-and-down emotional teeter-totter that causes much confusion in a once secure situation, especially for the nonquestioning spouse, who becomes more and more suspicious with every change of normal activity. The questioning spouse may even demand private time to make some important decisions that will affect both people's lives. It is not easy for one person to make decisions that will radically change the direction of a commitment made for what was to be for a lifetime. But this is exactly what is evolving—a decision that will affect not only the decision maker, but the spouse and a large number of other people who are associated with this marriage, including any children.

There is no specific timetable or length for this first phase of the divorce process. For some, the question of whether or not to continue in a relationship becomes a lifetime process that is never truly resolved. For others, closure to a relationship of many years might take only a year or so.

Nor must this questioning stage inevitably end in a decision to divorce. Separation or divorce is certainly the only option left when one or both spouses will not consider anything else. But if the decision is tentative on both sides, then there is a number of ways to keep the marriage intact. One of these might be the re-establishment of the communication skills that are necessary for any marriage to work. This can be accomplished with a skilled marriage counselor or other qualified person. (But the person must be truly qualified—by experience, or education, or both.). Many religious organizations also have programs which are directed toward enriching a marriage. But these types of programs must be honest enough to deal with all the options available to a marriage that is in trouble, including separation or divorce. They should not be programs based on the premise that a marriage has to stay intact at all costs. Some marriages need to be ended for the well-being of all parties involved.

The emotions of this questioning period are always difficult to contend with. Primary among them is guilt. The questioning spouse, as he or she arrives at a decision, sometimes seeks to ensure that the decision (and the perceptions that led to it) are fully shared by the other spouse, thus alleviating the guilt associated with being the decision maker. The questioner many times insists the relationship should end cleanly, leaving everyone involved friends. But it often doesn't take long for him or her to realize that the divorce will not be clean—it will be quite devastating and messy.

That realization is the end of the sort of innocent, self-absorbed first stage of divorce in which one spouse first questions the investment made in the marriage and then decides to end it, supported by the dreamy assurance that the other spouse will surely understand and not resist. Next comes the escape stage, the phase in which the decision needs to be communicated. This stage has its own unique possibilities for pain and anguish.

CHAPTER 2

THE ESCAPE STAGE

HOW DO I SAY IT'S OVER?

Martha's Story

I am a 33-year-old woman who has been married for seven years. I recently came to the conclusion, after a long time of uncertainty, that I no longer should be married to my husband. I am the type of person who wants things to be done correctly, and I felt guilty about making a unilateral decision. I really did enjoy and love Phil, but our relationship had grown so apart that it was really the last thing I wanted to work on. My career had become very important to me, and my self-confidence had grown over the years, so I felt I no longer needed—and also had outgrown—my husband. I had no way of knowing how to tell Phil what my feelings were, so I decided that acting out my feelings would force him to come to the same conclusion that I had arrived at. I started going out more often with people from work, even though I knew Phil disliked this and was somewhat of a jealous and possessive person. The more time I spent out, the more difficult things became and the guiltier I felt.

I told Phil that nothing was wrong, however, and that I just needed some time with my friends. Eventually my husband accepted this because he loved me and could not find any way of changing my mind. After a period of time, I started to take money out of my paycheck and spend it on things that I knew would annoy Phil. There were many things our family needed, and both of us had been saving up for these essentials in planning for a better future. So when I decided to spend money on myself and on nonessentials, our compromises became tense and the relationship strained. Our arguments eventually became more pronounced. We were forever bickering over money, outside involvements, and outside relationships.

At one point, word got back to Phil by way of some friends that I was seen with a certain guy more than a couple of times. This alerted Phil to the many unexplained charges that were showing up on our credit card bills. Phil sat down with me to discuss this whole matter. I became incensed, insisting that there was nothing going on with another guy and that I was feeling hemmed in by our marriage. Phil said he felt he was becoming a very desperate person, in the sense that he thought he had to put up with this stuff in order to keep me. This feeling of desperation and powerlessness made Phil more angry at himself than he was at me.

The whole situation began to create problems for Phil which spilled over into his job and business relationships. As for our marriage, it had been going nowhere in the last year. Phil eventually approached me, telling me that he did not like the changes in himself. He also said that I seemed very unhappy, he was really depressed, and both of us should do something about it. He suggested the two of us should see a counselor or a minister to assist us in getting our marriage back together, but I would have nothing to do with it. I told him whatever we had lost between us was not worth saving and in no way would I bring in a third party to try and solve our problems.

At this point, Phil made the final decision. He informed me that he wanted a divorce. My strategy succeeded.

Reflection

Most people think they would enjoy a life not filled with difficult questions that belabor their consciences. They adopt many strategies to avoid confronting moral complexities and the attendant conscience problems that follow. Guilt in the divorcing process is one of those complex questions. Honest guilt, an acknowledgment to self that wrong has been done, can bring out the best in a person and call him or her to make shared decisions with the other spouse. The couple will explore all avenues and, if separation and divorce is their joint decision, their separation can be relatively clean and peaceful. But neurotic guilt, unacknowledged and unaccepted, can bring out the worst in an individual. In a counterproductive state of guilt, priority is given not to the effort to deal with the things that bring about the guilt but to the effort to repress the guilt and ignore its causes.

Martha's is an example of one of the many poor strategies for dealing with the guilt of deciding to end a marriage. Her efforts to get her husband to share her view that their marriage was over created more pain in the long run than might have been caused by a straightforward admission of her intent. Her reasoning, were she to state it explicitly, went like this: "This marriage is over, but just bluntly announcing my intention to divorce would hurt Phil terribly. Getting involved with something or someone that my spouse will see as a clear threat to the marriage, however, will make it obvious to him that the marriage is over."

Martha's strategy for escape was to ask: "How do I get my spouse to come to the same conclusion I have?" This is a common goal in many divorces. Unfortunately, Martha's story is one of acting out of counterproductive guilt as an escape mechanism.

Today there are many, and often confusing, reasons for divorcing. People petition for a divorce because of boredom or the excitement of a career, because of too many children or no children. Some couples fail to understand the amount of work required to maintain a good marital relationship and are disillusioned when their marriage fails to "go by itself." People sometimes feel that they have outgrown their spouse or that their spouse has outgrown them. Some no longer want to be victim-ized in an abusive relationship, while others think they will be more comfortable in another relationship and end up leaving the healthy for the unhealthy. It could be said that there are as many reasons for divorcing as there are individuals who divorce. But there is one element which, when missing from a marriage, seems to create the atmosphere for divorce to take place, and that element is the lack of communication.

Communication is essential at every phase of a marriage. When two people do not talk to one another about themselves, they cease growing with each other and, equally important, stop discovering new things about each other that carry their relationship to new levels of intimacy. And intimacy in a marriage is the framework around which spouses create a family, whether that family embraces just two people or includes children and even other extended family members.

The reasons for divorce are unique to each couple, but they are not all valid. When the desire for divorce results from a simple failure to do the necessary work of intimacy, or from an immature set of expectations about marriage, divorce is the wrong answer to the problem. Such couples should seek ways to restore communication, to build intimacy with which they feel safe. All marriages need to be continuously worked at. The only time divorce should be considered is when differences are impossible to reconcile even though sincere efforts have been made or when the relationship has become destructive to one or both members.

Even in this escape stage of divorce, a marriage can still be rescued if both parties work at it in good faith. Skilled counseling is necessary to sort out, objectively, the problems that are going on in the relationship. These attitudes and behaviors usually need to be discussed by both spouses with the assistance and balancing influence of an outside party or parties. (A three-person team—both spouses and a trained counselor—seems to be the most beneficial situation during the first two stages of the divorcing process, the questioning phase and the escape phase. For most people, however, group or peer counseling seems to be more productive and effective during stages three and four, the transition phase and the rediscovery phase.)

Is there ever a time when the spouse who originally sought the divorce comes to the conclusion that this is not what he or she really wants? This happens quite often. But if that spouse has engaged in unhealthy guilty behavior like Martha's, usually the other spouse has been put through so much and feels so angry and violated that there is no turning back from the divorce process. The divorce has now truly become the decision of the other spouse.

There is a point in the divorce process when a final psychological or physical separation takes place. There is often one single statement that identifies and memorializes that separation. It is: "I called a lawyer today." Lawyers may already have been called a number of times with questions such as: "If I'm going to get a divorce, how much money will it cost?" or "If I'm going to get a divorce, how much time will it take?" But when one spouse finally says to the other, "I called a lawyer today," that means, "I don't want any more of the garbage that is going on in our lives. I want you out of my life because I'd be better off without you (and so would the children). This whole situation has caused me to be an angry, sad, and destructive person, and I don't like it." So a formal separation takes place and the third phase of the divorce process begins—the transition stage.

Chapter 3

The Transition Stage

Why Are The Walls Closing In On Me?

David's Story

I am 32 years old and have been divorced for three years. Divorcing was the most devastating thing that has ever happened to me. I really hope I never have to go through anything like it again. I also hope that not too many people have to endure the deep pain that goes along with this traumatic event.

I can remember everything like it was yesterday. My wife and I were having some major problems in our marriage. We had tried to work through them as best we could, but nothing seemed to help. We tried a marriage counselor, then a psychologist, and finally the pastor at our church. The more we talked, the more confused we got, the

more distant from each other we felt. Things never
turned better, only worse. At one point during one
of our many sessions, I don't remember which one,
the counselor suggested that maybe we could never
make things work between us. Maybe we had too
many differences that would keep us from living
with one another in a solid marriage. I remember
asking the question, "What about the nine years we
were married? For the most part things worked out
pretty good except for the last two years. And what
about the children?" (We have two boys and a girl.)
So, out of fear and desperation, we worked on it for
one more year before Liz finally filed for divorce.
She said she wanted to start life over again and do
the things she always wanted to do. There was
nothing I could do to stop her, and so we started
divorce proceedings.

At first, things went pretty calmly. We seemed
to be able to discuss the many questions involved
and make most of the decisions on our own. At that
point I wanted to make sure that Liz and the kids
were going to be taken care of. Then she dropped
the bomb. She wanted the house for herself, but she
had decided that I would have custody of the
children. I had taken for granted that she would
want the kids, and I had accepted that, even though

it would be very difficult for me. My immediate
question was very practical, "Where would the kids
and I live?" She was not sympathetic at all. She
said I made enough money to find another place and
raise the children with no difficulty. She wanted to
start all over without any "liabilities." This just
didn't sound like Liz. None of our friends or family
could understand what was going on in her mind. I
sure couldn't.

At that point we brought in the lawyers, and
for various reasons things became more difficult.
More and more decisions had to be made, which
caused more and more disagreements. There were
delays after delays in court, which caused further
disagreements, and finally hatred reared its ugly
head. Thus ended our comfortable and well-planned
divorce process!

After the ugly litigation, I felt psychologically
devastated and overwhelmed. There were times
when I felt like the walls were closing in on me. I
had very limited tolerance in dealing with any
problems that surfaced in my life or in the lives of
the kids. I just could not handle anything stressful.
I could not even deal with the usual stresses and
problems of everyday life. I felt easily over-

whelmed. And more often than I would like to admit, I felt like just ending everything and killing myself. Then there were more setbacks, and I would get even angrier at what my wife had done to us. My feelings would heat up and I would think up ways of killing her. Most of the time I would laugh at myself for these fantasies, but sometimes I would get scared because I thought I was taking them too seriously.

There were also times when I felt so alone and worthless that I didn't like myself. I knew no one wanted to be around a loser, but I tried going out on dates just to be with someone. It was hard getting back into that game, and I felt inept. I met a couple of women who were nice, but I became afraid of being hurt again and dropped them quickly. I needed someone to be with, but I was always afraid. I didn't want to get hurt, so I stayed to myself and plowed through living day by day. I would call my former wife often in those days. The excuse was to see if she was "OK." The real reason was that I was lonely and needed to hear her voice. I wished we could get back together, but that never entered her mind, or at least that's what she said.

By the time two years had passed after our divorce, however, things seemed to get better. I was no longer as stressed about everything. In fact I was doing very well—laughing more and going out with friends, both old and new. Many things were falling into place. The kids, who really took a back seat during all of this, were starting to bounce back, thanks to the help of some sensitive friends and relatives.

As more time passed, I began feeling more and more like myself. I was happy, successful, and felt pretty capable of handling just about anything. Eventually I felt so good about myself that I really felt capable of being happy without being married.

Reflection

David's story demonstrates the many psychological and emotional stages of the transition phase of divorcing. This third phase is the transition from being married to someone to being that person's adversary and, eventually, former spouse. It is during this third phase that one experiences the highest intensity of stress in the entire divorce process. Between the initial separation of the couple and the receipt of a final divorce decree, some form of litigation or legal procedures must take place. Because the duration of this legal work varies from state to state and case to case, it is impossible to predict with any precision the length of time it will take to complete a legal divorce or separation. It is also during this transition that a lot of destructive behavior—acting out, neurotic patterns, ugly confrontations—takes place in divorcing spouses' lives. Most people who are in divorce court are living in a state and quality of stress they have never experienced before and usually cannot handle well. An objective observer, watching the behavior of people in this stage, would at the very least think they need someone to talk to.

One young mother of three children said, "I went to the store on a Saturday. God knows why I went on a Saturday, anyway, because it seemed the entire world was at the same store that day. And here I am, trying to buy food for my three children and myself. I was loading the cart and my children were unloading it. I was putting their things back on the shelves and they were putting my things back. I was really becoming very frustrated with this whole scene. When I had finally completed my grocery shopping and had put everything in order, it took me 20 minutes to get to the cashier. I finally reached the checkout counter and everything seemed fine, but I started to cry for no reason at all. To this day, I do not know why I was crying except I suddenly had the feeling I was going to lose it all and have a nervous breakdown right there. And I just ran out of the store with my children, leaving the groceries in the cart."

The feeling that they are "going to lose it all" is one of the most frequently expressed reactions of people in divorce. As in David's case, there is constant fear of psychological breakdown. This is why divorcing people often become very self-protective. They build walls around themselves so they cannot get hurt by anyone, anymore, ever. Unfortunately, those walls often keep out the very people who can assist them in healing and learning to enjoy life again, comforting them through the sense of loss and grieving that comes with divorce.

People in the transition phase of divorce usually can't cope well with any stresses, neither their own nor those of their children. They either focus inward and become what appears to be selfish and self-centered, or focus outward, ignoring and repressing their feelings of loss and grief and becoming almost compulsively active and busy. It is important to know that these are survival techniques—not pleasant for family or friends to co-exist with—but only temporary responses to the overwhelming stress that has accumulated through the first three phases of divorce.

The question was once asked of a divorced or widowed support group: "Which do you think is more traumatic—losing a spouse by divorce or losing a spouse by death?" One woman responded, "I have been a widow for over two years. Since the day of my husband's death, I have been living a pure hell. That first year was unbelievable, and the second year was no better. It is only now that I am starting to live somewhat normally, beginning to understand and trust again, being my old self. It has taken me two and a half years to do it, but now I know I can make it. But I am not too sure I could deal with the situation that a friend of mine is in. She's been divorced as long as I have been wid-owed, and she is going through the same hell. But she will be going through it a lot longer than I will, for the mere fact that I was able to bury my husband's body and she wasn't. Her husband's body daily reappears in her life, opening up wounds, picking at the scab and starting it bleeding again. Every time she sees her husband—especially if he is with someone else—the jealousy of 'What does this other woman have that I don't? What can she do that I couldn't?' wells up again in her and a lot of anger and frustration just festers."

The protracted inability to "let go" of the former spouse is a common aftermath of divorce, and one that family and friends may not tolerate well as time goes on. Sometimes when it is literally impossible to avoid the constant reappearance of one's former spouse, a person may be compelled to move to another city (if there are no children or no custody and visitation barriers), or to change jobs or neighborhoods or churches in order to reduce the incidence of "accidental meetings." There are other behavior-modification techniques that can help with this situation and therapists who specialize in them.

Another frequent psychological reaction, as in David's case, is to consider suicide. Divorcing people may feel they want to end it all because "nothing is worth it anymore." They're embarrassed because they've been a "failure" in one of the most important relationships of adult life. In their youth, they dreamed of being married and living "happily ever after." This dream, once a reality, is no more. They not only feel alienated from their spouses, but also from society and even sometimes their churches. They also feel divided from their families and their friends, especially their married friends, who might be afraid of being accused of "choosing sides" or who might see a divorced couple as a threat to their own fragile marriage. They may no longer be invited to family dinners, because their relatives don't know what to talk about in their presence or feel "it will be too hard for Joe to be with happily married relatives." It's no wonder that a divorcing person can end up feeling the only way out of this situation is suicide.

Suicide is obviously not the answer. Yet suicidal thoughts and fantasies are very frequent for people going through a divorce, and these tendencies should be taken very seriously. It is not easy, but it is necessary, to confront such fantasies directly. Friends, relatives, or pastoral counselors should ask, "Are you thinking about suicide? Have you made a plan?" If the answer to these questions is yes, there should be immediate protective intervention.

Sometimes divorcing people, like David, have a high level of homicidal fantasies. One woman described it this way: "I pray in front of the statue of the Blessed Mother ever day. I know it's wrong, but I still do it. I pray to the Blessed Mother that a plane that my former husband is on will blow right out of the sky. The reason is that I think I could deal with his death, but I can't deal with this divorce." Many ex-spouses who have not yet learned to live with divorce have angry fantasies about the deaths of their former mates. These can be very frightening to the person who experiences them and can best be coped with in a peer support setting, where they lose their power.

Several tempting options occur to divorcing people—options that look good, that appear to be an improvement over the sadness, loneliness, frustration or sense of failure that often accompanies divorce. One tempting option is to return to the same unhappy situation the person fought to escape. The rationalization? "Because I know what type of a hell the past was, and I do not know what type of a hell the future is going to be." Looking to the future is often a very scary prospect for divorcing persons. But to go back to an addicted or abusive spouse without having actually changed anything in his or her behavior, for example, is the worst action one could take. An abusive spouse's sense of power and guilt are both fed by the "reconciliation," and the abuse may become worse, rather than better. And for an addict, the return of a spouse may mean a return of the enabling behavior that allowed the addict to deny his or her problem and even a possible intensification of the addict's problem.

Another tempting option is to try to keep the marriage together for the sake of the children. There is a humorous story about an 80-year-old couple who went to see their pastor to tell him they were getting a divorce. The pastor asked them why they were splitting up after 60 years of marriage. "We wanted to wait until the children died before we got a divorce," they said! Even though the story may be apocryphal, there is a certain ring of truth to the reasoning. Divorce does affect a couple's children, no matter their age. But to remain in a destructive relationship for the sake of the children, when the children are usually among the people being destroyed, makes no sense. (The effects of their parents' divorce on children will be taken up in more detail in Part Two of this book.)

A final tempting option during the transition phase is to attach oneself to someone of the opposite sex who seems stronger than oneself, who can help one get through the process, whose shoulder one can cry on, and with whom one can go dancing, have dinner, and maybe even enter into a romance. That person can make one feel beautiful or handsome and restore the sense that life and love are again possible. Until one can feel all of these things without *needing* to be in an exclusive, marital-type relationship, however, this kind of singular attachment may merely postpone the inevitable emotional "crash" that accompanies a divorce—and also isn't fair to the other person involved in the "rebound." The best remedy for the "people-hunger" that comes with the newly single life of divorce is usually a peer support group. Divorcing people need to be with others in the same situation so they can come to understand that all the things they are going through are not unique to themselves—that they are the common experiences of divorce. That insight alone adds support. It also helps to have survivors, people who have made it through the divorce process, describe how they dealt with it.

Unless divorcing people go through the transition stage by themselves in the midst of such peers (which means alone but along with a group of similarly situated people and *not* with one specific individual), they are vulnerable to entering the fourth and final phase of divorce, the rediscovery stage, without completing the process necessary to truly end their former marriages so they can get on with the rest of their lives.

CHAPTER 4

THE REDISCOVERY STAGE

I FEEL, FOR THE FIRST TIME, THAT I AM LIVING MY OWN LIFE

Ann's Story

It has been four years since my divorce. After all the pain and anger have been put into perspective, I feel that for the first time in my life I am strong and capable of living my life the way I want to. Life seems more in control, my control. After going through so much of the depression, guilt, and God knows what else, I know that I can make it. I'm happy and satisfied with all that I've done and what I've set out to do. I'm not depending on anyone to protect me or give me security. I've learned to do that on my own. The seemingly insurmountable problems that I had have been worked out. Maybe not the way I originally wanted them to, but in the long run for the better.

I've also decided that I do not *have* to be married to be happy or successful. But at the same time I feel that I *want* to be married. I went through periods of hating all men, because I believed that all men were like my former husband. In some cases that's true, but for the most part they're not. But I also have come to the conclusion that maybe my former spouse and I are both "OK" people, but not "OK" for each other.

My life has changed so much for the better. I am stronger and more independent, which gives me a sense of balance. I am developing a value system which is more considerate and less self-centered. These qualities are new to me, because I never had time as I was growing up—especially while I was married—to develop them. There were too many other things that took priority. Now I feel I'm becoming the person I should be. I'm in a relationship with a man right now. It is very new, but it's the first one in which I don't feel desperate. If it works out I'll be delighted, but I'm not pushing anything. I'm still cautious about getting involved with anyone. I don't want to go through the same thing again.

Overall, I am a happier person now than I've ever been. And I know that I survived something that I wouldn't wish on my worst enemy.

Reflection

There is one statement that identifies the movement from the third to the fourth stage of the divorcing process, and that is, "I do not need to be married to be happy." If people have validly experienced that insight and can verbalize it, then they are into the fourth and final phase: rediscovery. This final stage is called rediscovery because it involves a regrounding of the individual in his or her sense of self—a reclaiming of values, attitudes, and life stance that arises out of his or her own inner authority.

Tangible evidence of rediscovery occurs when individuals not only resume responsibility for the old stresses in their lives but start to take on new ones, such as a new job, new lifestyle, or new relationships. People in the fourth stage of divorce are not as desperate as they used to be. Statements such as, "I am succeeding, I am doing well; I have a value system that is all mine and I know that I do not need to be married to have these things, or to make it in life, or to be successful," are evidence of rediscovery.

People like Ann should have been able to make these statements before they got married the *first* time. If that attitude were a requirement for first marriages, there would be a much better chance of first marriages succeeding. People often get married for the wrong reasons. They marry because they think the new mate is going to complete their lives in ways that they feel incapable of securing on their own—protection, security, home, children, whatever it is. In and of themselves, these needs might not be dangerous. But when they become *reasons* for a person to get married, they are the wrong way for a relationship to begin.

Likewise, many people who experience a second divorce started their second relationship before they successfully completed the rediscovery phase—either while they were still questioning their first marriage or were still escaping or transitioning out of their first marriage. Most of them married immediately after receiving the divorce decree from their first marriages. Such "rebound" marriages carry a very high risk of failure—much higher than even the risk of divorce in a first marriage.

This indicates that one has to get through the entire divorce process before committing oneself to another intimate relationship, or else the chance of another traumatic divorce is unacceptably high. A premature second marriage—to try taking all the pain away from a recent divorce—may turn out to be a source of new pain for both parties involved.

This raises an obvious question: "How long should a divorced person wait for a new love, a new marriage?" If it is, in fact, necessary to work through all four stages of divorce, it is hard to predict. Each person will take different amounts of time with each phase. To progress from escape through rediscovery may take several years and often longer—sometimes as long as 20 years. Some people never even reach rediscovery but become "stuck" in one of the earlier phases. For most people, the transition stage is often the place in which they get trapped, unable to let go of their former spouse, unable to accept the fact that each other's lives must move on. If this is the case, then it is folly even to consider entering into a second relationship until this roadblock has been dealt with.

A person who is unable to achieve the kind of rediscovery which will permit a new marriage with a high probability of success must be open to another option. Perhaps if the pressure to marry again were removed through the consideration of this option, real rediscovery might occur.

This option is a conscious decision to live as a single person, treating it with the same serious reflection as one would give to marriage. It used to be that single people were thought to be odd, or leftover, or in some way antisocial. But in our contemporary society, the idea of remaining single is very acceptable. Statistics indicate that there are significant numbers of people—divorced, widowed, and never married—who have made a very clear statement that they wish to live the rest of their lives as successful human beings without being married. This is a healthy choice, and one which ought to be encouraged and supported.

But for the vast majority of divorced people, another marriage will be the lifestyle of choice. This also can be a very healthy choice. The person contemplating another marriage must first suffi-ciently deal with the issues or problems in the previous marriage that created the atmosphere in

which the divorce became inevitable. Sufficient
time between the ending of an old relationship and
the beginning of a new one must also be given
serious consideration. Thirdly, the baggage of a
previous marriage must not be brought into the
development or the goals of a subsequent marriage.
Keeping these simple but difficult rules in mind may
help a person not only learn from the first marriage,
but also succeed at a new one.

Divorce does turn lives upside down, but—
whether one remarries or remains single afterward—
it is survivable.

Part II

THE EFFECTS OF DIVORCE ON

THE COUPLE'S CHILDREN

INTRODUCTION

What do children experience while their parents are going through a divorce? Note the phrase: "while their parents are going through a divorce." It is inaccurate and incomplete. Children do not experience their parents' divorce only while the parents are going through the divorce process. They do so over and over again throughout their lives. The effects of a divorce on a couple's children do not necessarily begin or end with the divorce decree or even the rediscovery stage of the parents. Certain challenges connected to the divorce will emerge in their lives as long as they, now grown to young adulthood and beyond, are involved in establishing and living in intimate relationships of their own.

The question is often asked: "Is a child ever too young to be aware of the problems of divorce or too old to experience its consequences?" The answer, of course, is no. Children in the womb feel the divorce trauma of their mothers. Children who are 30 or 40 years old at the time of their parents' divorce will still experience the results of that divorce in their own personal lives.

One woman was divorced when the youngest of her seven children was not yet two. It's not at all unusual for a boy that age to spend a great deal of his time with his mom, and so the divorce did not seem to affect him too much. When he began school, cub scouts, and little league, however, there were many dads involved. This young boy now felt the pain of not having his dad around all the time. For him the process of dealing with his parents' divorce did not begin immediately, but it would continue throughout his life. An example of this was his high school graduation. Whom should he invite, where should they sit, with whom should he celebrate afterwards? The process of adjusting to a parental divorce sometimes continues long after it has ceased to be an issue for the parents themselves.

Does this mean children of divorced couples are doomed for life? Absolutely not! It merely means that adults need to recognize the turmoil divorce can cause in children of all ages. The following stories and reflections seek to describe the effects of divorce on children during each of their four stages of dealing with the divorce of their parents.

Divorce is survivable for children, too, if they are given support, encouragement and love. For each painful situation they survive, they will be better equipped to handle the next challenge. If they handle it right, they will move into adulthood as successful, empathic, loving men and women— possibly better equipped for marriage then their parents ever were.

CHAPTER 5

THE CHILD'S QUESTIONING STAGE

WHY ARE THINGS BEGINNING TO CHANGE IN OUR FAMILY?

Mark's Story (told at age 27)

I really was very happy during the years that my folks were married. Life was as good for me as it was for my friends. When I was little, Mom and Dad seemed to enjoy each other, and we had a great deal of fun doing the things we did as a family. Vacations were really our best family time. Dad didn't have work on his mind, and Mom could relax and not worry about the house, and us, and keeping things in order. Those were the times when we most enjoyed being a family.

As we kids got older (there were three of us), however, I started to resent going on vacation with my family. There were friends of mine who would take trips with each other's families, and they seemed to have a lot more fun then we did. But no matter how often I brought up the idea of going on trips with other families, or having other kids come with us, Dad would always turn it down. Mom seemed to be open to the possibility, and so did my brother and sister, but it never caught on with my dad.

Dad was never the type of person to have a lot of people around. Come to think of it, I'm not sure he had any friends. Mom was the person who enjoyed talking with other people and would always laugh and have fun. Dad seemed to be annoyed with Mom when she would make new friends. But it never seemed to cause much difficulty between them.

The first time that I noticed things were different between them was when I was in eighth grade. Mom suddenly seemed less affectionate toward Dad than I was accustomed to seeing. Before this, when Dad would kid around with Mom, she would cuddle up with him and pretend to be hurt. But now she would just ignore him and continue doing what she was doing. Dad seemed to just shrug it off and change the subject. I thought that was odd.

As time went on, our family life became more and more quiet. There weren't as many fun times. And there seemed to be something changing that I just couldn't figure out. I thought maybe it was just that we were growing up and growing older. I never realized until much later that Mom and Dad were having problems—and those problems were the beginning of what ended up in their divorce.

Reflection

The first stage of the divorcing process as it affects children like Mark is usually not a lengthy process. Neither is it necessarily a tragic situation for the children. Since most often only one of the two spouses is involved in questioning a continuing investment in the marriage, there generally doesn't seem to be anything out of the ordinary on the surface of the family relationships. Still, a sensitive child can pick up something that seems new and negative in the emotional climate of the family, as was the case in Mark's story.

As this sense that something is different grows in intensity, the child himself or herself begins to question. What is going on in my parents' lives? My mother and father used to be more romantic. They did things with one another more often. They were more affectionate with one another. All of these things seems to be disappearing from their lives. Why? The child is not really demanding answers at this point, just asking questions.

Most questions at this stage would be laughed off by the parents anyway. Regardless of the state the couple is in, they don't want to upset their children. "Of course everything is fine, what could possibly be wrong?" "Nothing to worry about." "Just fine, Honey, everything is just fine." These are the answers children often hear over and over again, until one day they are told one of their parents has moved out of their house. This is one of the reasons divorce seems so sudden and unexpected to children. The two people they loved and trusted most in the world are separating, and no one will even tell them why.

Although not much can be done at this stage to explain to children what is going on in the marriage (since the parents often don't know themselves), later on the reasons for the divorce need to be dealt with in a manner appropriate to the age of each child.

There are whole sections of books in the library to help children of all ages understand divorce. (*Kids are Nondivorceable* and *Teens are Nondivorceable* are two versions of the same excellent workbook by Sara Bonkowski aimed at helping divorcing parents deal with their own children about the divorce.*) There are even picture books for the youngest of children that help parents explain why Mom or Dad are no longer living together. Numerous games are available that a parent can play with children or adolescents, each geared to enhancing communication and understanding between family members.

Nothing, however, can take the place of simple, open communication between parent and child, even in the first, questioning stage of divorce. It becomes even more important in the second stage, which for the child is *anti*-escape.

*(1987, 1990, ACTA Publications, Chicago, Illinois)

CHAPTER 6

THE CHILD'S ANTI-ESCAPE STAGE

HOW DO I GET MOM AND DAD TO TALK TO ONE ANOTHER AGAIN?

Renee's Story (TOLD AT AGE 30)

The first time I heard my father and mother discuss divorce was during one of their "quiet" arguments. I'm not sure if they had made a final decision about getting a divorce, but it eventually ended up as one. That possibility really scared me into trying to patch up their marriage as much as I could. When I first heard the word "divorce," I became very light-headed and even nauseated. I remember too much coming to my mind at the same time. I didn't know what to do. During the following days, I thought about many things that had happened over the past couple of years—events that happened or words that were used that I only then realized were the prelude of what was happening and what was to follow.

I was a very creative child. And many of the things that were happening to me at that time, I felt, needed to be dealt with creatively. I was a very good student. My mother and father prided themselves on the fact that their daughter was an "A" student and could still handle a number of extra-curricular activities. I decided that the best way to bring them back together was to create some worries in the one area in which they both found mutual pride . . . me.

So I started to slack off on my homework and not to involve myself so much in events after school. I started this slowly, so as not to be obvious. My teachers didn't notice my retreating for a couple of weeks. When it became obvious to them, one of them asked to see me. I wasn't totally open with him, but I knew that he could see right through me. The more I pulled away, the more teachers began to comment. During physical education class, I would not give it all that I could. I would sometimes sit events out, faking sickness or forgetfulness. I would be late for class and joke about it, which caused more teachers' concern.

Finally, my mother told me that she received a call from my homeroom moderator and was asked to come in along with my father to talk over this change in me. I was relieved and concerned at the same time. I wasn't sure if it was going to work, but I knew I was doing everything I could. But "everything I could" was not enough. After a couple of months of worrying more about me than about themselves, they announced they were filing for a divorce. My strategy—and my world—crumbled.

Reflection

When the escape stage of the disinvesting parent begins, the lives of the children dramatically change. They begin to see the fights, notice one of the parents staying away from home more often, feel the urge to take sides. Suddenly, there is chaos in the home. And just as suddenly, the children are thrust into the divorcing process.

Children are far too often placed in the middle of the divorce because each parent looks to the children to side with him or her. The parents seek a child's attention, vying for affection and beginning, subtly, to preview the single-parent families that will eventually emerge from the wreckage. The children's reaction is two-folded: (1) they feel responsibility (and therefore guilt) for what is happening, and (2) like Renee, they begin to try, in ways that vary with the age of the child, to cure the situation before a separation or divorce can actually happen.

Just as a parent's escape strategy can be acted out in many different ways, children often adopt a variety of "anti-escape" strategies of their own—getting Mom and Dad together again by creating some common area of concern, for example. Teachers are often the first to see a dramatic change in behavior when a child's strategy begins. Renee, who used to do well in the classroom, who was faithful with her homework, and who was very attentive and sociable, suddenly no longer functioned well. Sometimes children become very unsociable—standing alone at the periphery of the playground, becoming the class clown or even the class bully. Such children—whether aware of it or merely acting out of their own depression or anxiety—are developing a strategy to prevent or delay a parent's escape from the marriage, often recruiting teachers and school to help carry it out.

The child in the anti-escape stage mirrors, in a nonarticulate way, the tension, anger, and acting out of the parent in his or her escape phase. What the child is silently pleading is, "Take a look at how differently I am acting, how differently I am feeling. Help me. Do something about it. Stay together."

So the school calls in the mother and father for a conference to talk about the child and how much he or she has changed. Sometimes one or both of the parents are aware of the changes in the child; sometimes, sadly, both parents are so focused on their own survival that they have not recognized what is happening to their own child. It becomes, then, the responsibility of teachers, ministers and others who have contact with children to support and assist the family by supporting and assisting the child. They must be alert to the anguish behind such changes in behavior, which can take various forms and expressions. Children are often calling out for help because they feel helpless and incapable of living with the tension in their homes much longer.

Those who would help the children of divorce need to become aware of the problems experienced by children of divorce, to learn to support and assist without interfering or taking sides, to avoid being pulled into the system of blame and guilt that operates in such families, and to allow these children some leeway to express their anger and grief and fear.

Parents, for their part, need to be as sensitive as possible—given their own problems—to their children's needs. Parents need to open lines of communication with their children about what is happening to their family. Outside help may be needed to accomplish this task.

If this is true in the first two stages of divorce, it is even more crucial in the third, the transition stage.

CHAPTER 7

THE CHILD'S TRANSITION STAGE

NO VOICE, NO CHOICE

Tom's Story (TOLD AT AGE 21)

I remember when I only wanted to be called Thomas. I needed to feel grown up. It was important to me then and probably was both good and bad. That was the time when my mother and father had split, and our family was never to be the same. It seems so many years ago, yet it also feels like it was yesterday. I know I sound confused. I still am, 11 years later.

Coming from a divorced home (I know that sounds funny, but it was just that) wasn't the greatest experience in my life. But, then again, it wasn't the worst. Sure it was devastating and there were many times I thought I wouldn't make it, but I did, only to realize I would have to deal with many of the same problems later in my own relationships.

Let me tell you what happened.

I was ten years old when my parents divorced.
I was not sure why they divorced, and to this day
they have never really talked about the reasons. As
long as I could remember, they had fought a lot and
never really seemed to be in love with each other. I
don't think I ever saw them hold hands, much less
kiss. They never showed any affection to any of us
children, either, but I just took that as being normal.
I noticed parents of some of my friends saying nice
things to each other or kidding around and even
kissing, but I just thought that was because they
were Italian or something!

The day my dad was served the divorce papers,
I was home watching TV. He had already moved
out of the house a couple of months before. I was
angry at both of them, but especially Mom. I just
figured she could have done more to save the
marriage. She was ruining not only Dad's life, but
also her kids'. Dad called that day to talk to Mom.
She wasn't home, so he unloaded on me. I remember I wanted to scream, but nothing would come out.
My throat was closing in and I ached with tears, but
I couldn't make a sound. I wanted to run away, but
I couldn't move from the chair. I was frozen.

Finally, Dad hung up and I just sat there trying not to cry. I remember being afraid and insecure. If Mom got rid of Dad so fast, how long would it be before she threw me out? Or worse yet, maybe she would pack up and leave us. I began staying awake late into the night, thinking that if Mom tried to leave I would stop her or go with her. I felt so lost.

My fear then turned into anger. I began to hate both my folks and was getting to hate all adults. I would scream and cry, give my mother the silent treatment, or just become nasty and call her really terrible names. (I discovered later that was probably one of the healthiest things I could have done, but maybe not in those exact ways. I needed to get rid of my hurt and anger.) I also didn't feel life was worth it anymore. Several times I thought about killing myself. Those were very serious times for me.

As time went on, life became even more difficult. We couldn't have all the things we used to have. Money was short, and life wasn't fun anymore. Mom was depressed all the time. I suppose she must have wondered over and over if she had done the correct thing in divorcing Dad. She was trying to find some way to get out of her depressions, but nothing seemed to help. She dated a number of guys, but she didn't like any of them. She referred to them as "animals." Nothing seemed to go right for her, and the effects of her disappointment ruled the house. There were many times when she tried to deal with her children's feelings and behaviors, but she just couldn't follow through. She would always end up crying. This made us even more uncomfortable and angry, because it made us feel totally helpless and completely responsible at the same time.

Life began to get better after two or three years. I finally decided to speak to someone I could trust. I realized I couldn't do that with Mom, because she was having such difficulty with her own problems and I didn't want to burden her with mine. After talking a lot of things out with a good friend and unloading on him all the guilt, suicidal feelings, anger, and other things I felt, we both concluded the best thing for me to do was to see someone who could give professional help. I was really scared and felt embarrassed to see a counselor, but it turned out to be the best thing I could have done for myself.

From that time on I was involved in a therapy group with kids very much like me. I had always thought I was the only one who felt all those ugly things—that I was the only one who felt I was hanging on a bar upside down and trying to live my life from that perspective. The group helped me feel normal again, to know that all the feelings that had been part of my life for all these years were the same ones most of the other kids were feeling too. It felt good to be one of a group again . . . not just someone sitting on the sidelines feeling different and alone.

About the same time that Mom was getting back to some normalcy, I began feeling pretty good about myself and became determined not to let my folks' divorce of each other divorce me from them. I love them both—and not unlike Mom and Dad—I finally wanted to get on with my life.

Reflection

During their parents' transition stage—while the separation and divorce are actually taking place—children like Tom experience many of the same psychological problems their parents do. Many children become extremely insecure at this point. They have no voice and no choice in what is happening. They sometimes begin to deal with some fearsome questions: "If Dad left us, how long will it be before Mom does too?" "If Mom hates Dad, how long will it be before she hates us?" These children lived in a home that used to be "good enough" for them, even though there were problems. Or perhaps they didn't even realize there were problems. Now they are suddenly living in a single-parent home, and the other parent is no longer there. Some children don't understand this change and think that from now on only one parent will take care of them, feed them, clothe them, and love them. Some even fear that love is not a sure thing anymore because, "I might come home one day after school and my Mom or Dad might be gone too." How do children act out this insecurity?

When one woman was divorced, she found it very difficult to get all her children off to school and herself off to work each morning. No matter how well she planned, one daughter would phone her during the day to say she forgot her sweater or her lunch or her homework. Each day there was another reason requiring the woman to drop off something for her daughter at school. Finally, when the woman made it quite clear to the girl that she was not going to bring anything else to school under any circumstances, the child began going to the classrooms of her brothers and sisters everyday asking for a pencil or part of their lunches. Many of the teachers in the school were becoming upset with the girl, but no one could make her stop these activities. No one seemed to realize that what the child was doing was checking. There were six people in her family when she left for school in the morning. How many would there be when she got home? Her Dad was gone; who else was going to leave?

This is just one of the ways a child will act out the insecurity caused by parental divorce during the transition stage. Children in divorcing families also sometimes become very angry people. The murderous feelings parents have as they move through a divorce manifest themselves in different ways in the children. As in Tom's case, they become so angry at both parents for changing their lives so drastically that they lash out—sometimes verbally, sometimes physically. Children will attack not only their parents, but anyone who seems to symbolize their parents. They are demonstrating the pain they are feeling in their changed lives.

Like all children, children of divorce—especially teenagers—can become suicidal. A number of children of divorce seem to be ending their lives because they cannot deal with their parents' divorces. There is no way that we can be positive as to the reason or reasons for a particular suicide, but a parent, teacher, or minister who ignores the classic signs of suicidal intent in any child is making a serious mistake, including when the child seems upset or depressed because of a parental breakup.

Children will seek out people who can help them with their problems, as Tom eventually did. Because they are a part of the daily lives of their students, educators are a prime choice, but friends, ministers, and other relatives are also chosen. Children often attempt to form temporary support-seeking relationships with others because their parents are at the time incapable of dealing effectively with the children's stresses. So sometimes children approach those adults who appear most open, most able to understand and listen, and most nonjudgmental.

Such a relationship is usually short-lived and must remain confidential. Children will describe the awful things that are going on at home to these outsiders, asking questions and seeking some direction on how they should act. If whatever is confided in such conversations does get back to the parent or parents, then the trust relationship is broken and there is no way to repair it. (If a child talks of suicide, that, of course, must be relayed to the appropriate authorities, including the parents, but the confidentiality of the relationship can still be maintained by telling the child why it must be done and accompanying him or her through the intervention.)

A confidant of a child of divorce must never be judgmental about what the child's mother or father is doing. This trusted person must never take sides or attempt to judge who is right or wrong. The children will only resent such judgments from an outsider. Children usually need this type of outside support for only a finite period of time. When balance returns to their lives, they will move on and become less dependent on outsiders.

By listening carefully and sensitively to what a child is saying, a confidant can sense the time when it is appropriate to lead the child back to a renewed relationship with his or her parents. This can usually happen once the parents have entered the rediscovery stage of the divorce process, when the dust has settled and mother and father can become effective parents again. (Note: A nonprofessional confidant may have questions about how to handle this situation and may even encounter resentment from one or both parents. The best thing to do in this case is for the confidant to seek and follow advice from a trained counselor.)

Yet another reaction of children in both the transition and rediscovery phases is to try to marry off one or both parents as soon as possible. Older children especially fear, in only a semi-humorous way, that they are going to be stuck taking care of their mother or father if he or she does not remarry!

One woman told this humorous story of her children's attempt to marry her off. At the time, she had been divorced for 17 years, yet she was still in the process of raising her seven children on her own. (At the time of her divorce, her youngest child had been a year old.) To make ends meet, this woman had three jobs. One of the jobs was at a flower shop, where she often made floral arrangements with a candle in the center for parties. When the parties were over, she would take home the used candles. Around Christmastime she would melt down all the colorful candles, make Christmas candles, and give them away as gifts. One morning when she was leaving for work she told her children she had invited a gentleman from her office to stop in for a drink after work and that they were planning to go out to dinner afterwards.

Her plans changed during the day, however, and she came home alone. When she opened the door to the house she found all of her children in order of size, sitting on the living room couch watching television and wearing their Sunday best. Then she noticed that the house was suffused with an eerie glow. As she walked from room to room, she realized that on every flat surface—including the back of the toilet!—was a lighted candle. The children had put candles in cups, candles on plates . . . . There were burning candles everywhere.

It looked, she said, like a cross between Halloween and midnight Mass. The children had tried to make the place so romantic that this gentleman would be moved to sweep their mother off her feet, marry her, and take them all away to live happily ever after!

Sometimes the opposite is true. Sometimes children are adamantly opposed to having anyone else come into their mother's or father's life and automatically dislike the people their parents are dating. This is especially true in the transition phase, and often for good reason: first experiments with dating often occur during people's nuttiness time in the divorce process, and their dating choices are far from what their choice would be once their self-esteem returns. One woman once said it was like having five fathers instead of five sons when her dates arrived. As soon as the doorbell rang, they were all there to greet the poor man: "How many miles do you run each day?" "How many chin ups can you do?" "What's the batting average of . . . ." On and on they went until the final blow: "Why don't you have any hair?" It wasn't that her sons intensely disliked any of these men. They merely felt a responsibility to protect their mom. Perhaps deep in their hearts they believed that if they could keep her from liking another man, then maybe someday their dad could come back home.

Many of the trials and tribulations children bombard their parents with following a divorce have that underlying hope of reunification: "If I cause enough trouble in school and Mom and Dad both have to see the principal . . ." or "If I'm sick enough that Mom and Dad both have to see the doctor . . . ." No matter what the scheme, the end result in the child's mind is that it will require Mom and Dad to be in the same room together where, upon seeing each other, they will immediately make up and get back together.

Many times children are truly very worried about their parents. Because the parents are viewed by them as unstable, children feel they must protect their parents. Many children become very compassionate and understanding and take on the role of parenting the parent. Concerned relatives and friends of the newly divorced often go to the oldest child and say, "You're the man of the house now, take care of your mom," or "Your mom doesn't live here any longer and as the oldest girl you have to take care of the household, it's your job now."

Another psychological dilemma children often face in the transition phase—and it is something the parents have to sit down with their children and discuss openly and early on—is the question of guilt. Whose fault was it? Children can blame themselves for the divorce: "It was something that I didn't do, or the way that I did something, that caused my mother and father to divorce."

One 17-year-old young man told this story: "I really have always blamed myself for my mother and father's divorce. When I was born, I supposedly was a surprise. It was an accident. I remember my mother and father and my sisters telling me stories of how well things were going prior to my birth. After I was born, there was an extra financial burden on my father, so he had to go and find a second job to support the family. In the midst of that turmoil and tension, he started to drink quite a bit—so much so that Mom and Dad argued more often, which resulted in the divorce." This young man's logic was that if he hadn't been born, his father would not have had to get the second job, the drinking would never have been a problem, the arguments would not have happened, and there would not have been a divorce.

In trying to spare a child as much pain as possible, Mom will often say, "Your Dad is really a good father and he loves you very much, but Mom and Dad just can't live together anymore." Dad will say, "Your Mom is really a great mother and she really loves you, but Mom and Dad just can't live together anymore." Children then have to figure out why two people, who think so much of each other, can't make their marriage work. Sometimes children blame themselves, especially if they hear their parents arguing about things that concern the children. Children will readily accept unrealistic guilt and try repeatedly to make up for their mistakes.

This is why children of all ages need to be told something about why parents are divorcing. There is, however, a very fine line between "something the child needs to know" and "something a parent needs to tell the child." A child needs and wants to love both parents—good, bad, or indifferent. Bad mouthing an ex-spouse only hurts children more deeply. In explaining a divorce to children, parents must be truthful but also sensitive to each child's age and the need for children to continue to love both parents.

Understanding parental divorce is not an easy task. It often takes years or professional help to accomplish. Still, it is critical to the successful completion of children's transition stage. Only then can they go on with their lives.

For in contrast to parents, who need to leave their past marriage behind, children need to retain the past in healthy and growth-enabling ways. Many children, of course, want to recapture the intact family, with Mom and Dad together in a happy home and living happily ever after. That, in most cases, will not occur. But what they can and need to do is rediscover something more basic in their life situation, which they can only do in the fourth and final phase in the divorce process, the rediscovery stage.

CHAPTER 8

THE CHILD'S REDISCOVERY STAGE

WILL MY PARENTS' HISTORY REPEAT ITSELF?

Patricia's Story (told at age 38)

My parents divorced 20 years ago, when I was 18. Time has really healed many of the old wounds and confusion. I remember knowing full well that the decision they made concerning their divorce was the right one. We all knew the fighting, jealousy, and craziness that had become part of our family life was not normal and had become very dysfunctional, but we didn't know the terminology to identify it. We thought that the act of divorcing would cure all the ills and that we could all get on with our own lives. But that's not how becoming adjusted to a divorce happens. Sure, we were dealing with the emotions that went with breaking up a family that had been together, at least physically, for a long time. But we didn't expect the various other emotions that followed our rational acceptance of the divorce decree.

I remember becoming very closed-in and self-protective. This was not my usual behavior pattern, but it felt comfortable and allowed me to start thinking more about myself. This stage, I remember, lasted for some time. Eventually I noticed that I was spending too much time alone. I realized immediately what I had done—I had needed the time alone to catch up with all that had happened, emotionally and not just intellectually. And that was good. But once I had accomplished that "catching up," too much time alone was no longer beneficial.

Another thing I noticed as time went on was my cautiousness toward men I dated. I did not want to get involved, nor did I expect to get serious with anyone, until I was certain that the relationship would be "healthy." There always seemed to be a flaw in every one of the guys I dated. Either he was too possessive, or not possessive enough. There was a lack of maturity, or he was out of my league. He drank too much, or he never let his hair down. I was always finding excuses for not going out with the same person more than once. This got to be depressing, and I needed to talk to someone about the whole thing.

My mother and I sat down one night to discuss it. She had recovered from the emotional setbacks of the divorce by then, and she was capable of helping me without bringing her agenda into the process. That conversation, plus the several that followed, were helpful and full of insights. By talking honestly with Mom I discovered more about myself, what I was doing, and how overly cautious I had become.

By this time, my mother had been seeing a particular man on a regular basis, and their relationship was becoming very serious. Mother brought to my attention that I was not very friendly to him and that maybe we should also talk about that. I honestly never realized how cold I was being toward this man, and I was floored to hear how I had been acting toward him. I was obviously protecting myself from being hurt again by not allowing anyone to come into my life who could possibly become important to me. There was also a feeling of jealousy toward my mother's friend. It surfaced the more she and I talked. I was feeling resentful that someone was coming into her life and stealing her away from me.

Now I'm married and have a family of my own. It has not been easy. There were times when I thought that my marriage was becoming exactly the same as my parents', and I wanted to get out of it as quickly as possible. But some good friends helped me put my marriage in perspective. My marital problems were *nothing* like those of my parents, but they *were* like those of other married couples who were trying to adjust as two individuals coming together to create a marriage while still trying to retain their own individuality.

Reflection

What happens to children when parents move from the transition into the rediscovery stage? Some, like Patricia, become very fearful and very jealous. If a new relationship is beginning between a parent and someone else, children will often test that relationship to its extremes to see if it is good for the parent and good for themselves. The way children do that is to challenge and question, critique and argue with the parent—and also with the new "significant person."

Children also become upset at this stage because as parents were going through the divorcing process they might not have had the energy to give each child adequate time and care. Now that life is better for Mom and Dad, they have more energy but someone else is getting the benefit of their new, happy, peaceful disposition.

As in Patricia's case, sometimes a child fears that "If I allow myself to fall in love and marry, history will repeat itself and I will be hurt again." Unfortunately, that might happen. Although a couple that chooses to divorce does not inevitably cause their children to divorce, the fact of the matter is simply this: children raised in a single-parent home usually spend more time choosing a spouse but less time trying to make their marriage work than those from intact two-parent families. Children of divorce often see divorce as one of the equally available and acceptable options to ending an unsatisfactory relationship. They've been through a divorce, they've seen their parents survive it, and they know they can too. They can be unwilling to deal with any long-term pain in a relationship and want out of the marriage at the first sign of difficulty. They also are sometimes afraid of arguing with their spouse and don't understand that a healthy disagreement can be a positive experience. At the first signs of discontent, they think divorce.

On the other hand, there are others who, having been brought up in a single-parent home, are bound and determined never to divorce. They know firsthand what divorce does to a family. They know exactly what it is like to have a parent leave home. They will try continually to keep their marriage intact—even if their efforts are counterproductive.

So, does divorce breed divorce in the next generation? Not necessarily. It can be used as an excuse or a blueprint by children in their own marriages, or it can provide them with greater insight and understanding of what it takes to make a marriage work.

The choice of how they will react in their own marriages is, ultimately, that of the children of divorce. If they can successfully complete their own rediscovery stage of their parents' divorce process, these children can have as good a chance at successful relationships and marriage as anyone.

In her process of rediscovery, Patricia had to deal first with her own reaction of turning inward. Then she had to come to the realization (with her mother's help) of how she was shutting other people out of her life. Finally married herself, she had to come to grips (again with the help of friends) with the fact that her marriage—like every marriage—has problems, but that she could not blame her parents' divorce for those problems.

For children of divorce, as for the divorcing couple themselves, divorce does turn lives upside down. But it is survivable!

OTHER BOOKS ON DIVORCE

Kids Are Nondivorceable and *Teens Are Nondivorceable* by Sara Bonkowski. Two versions of a workbook designed to help parents deal with their children about the parents' divorce. $5.95 each.

Divorce and Beyond by James Greteman and Leon Haverkamp. A group program for newly divorced persons focuses on the "mourning period" of the divorce process. Participant's books and facilitator's manuals are $4.95 each.

Available through most Christian bookstores or call 800-397-2282